I0789629

I Don't Want To Be Bad

A CBT Workbook for Kids, Parents, and Professionals who Help Them

Amy Marschall, Psy.D.

This book was published thanks to free support and training from:

TCKPublishing.com

Special thank you to my husband, Michael, for his help in editing this manuscript. I love you!

In my time as a psychologist, I have met with hundreds of kids. These kids have come from all kinds of homes, family systems, and backgrounds, and they present with all kinds of challenges. The one thing they have in common is that, deep down, every single child *wants to be good*. Do they act out to get adults' attention? Absolutely! Do they choose frustrating behaviors because they don't know better? For sure! Kids need interaction, and making adults angry is often the fastest way to get it.

So how can we, the adults, help children learn how to manage and communicate their emotions appropriately? Helping parents answer that question is the reason I wrote this book.

This workbook is created for use by professionals who work with children with emotional and behavioral issues and the adults who love and care for those children. It is intended for use in a clinical context, by teachers who are trying to implement trauma-informed resources in their classroom, or by parents who want to implement the tools with their kids at home.

The activities and tools provided are designed for children from approximately age 5-12, although teens could also benefit from these skills. These tools are presented to help kids learn self-regulation, mindfulness, and communication of feelings. The order provided is intended to allow both parents and children to build upon skills they have already learned. However, professionals and parents can use their discretion about what tools will be most helpful at a given time. This book is designed to help kids get in touch with their feelings and share these feelings in an appropriate and effective way.

Although this book was written with kids with mental health challenges in mind, many of these activities can benefit anyone! What child hasn't had a day when they need to focus on slowing down and taking big breaths?

The book starts with tools to help parents implement these skills in their home, then introduces relaxation exercises to help kids calm their bodies when they are escalated. It progresses into teaching them how to identify what is going on inside of their bodies, even when they might not have a specific name for that feeling. Next, it helps kids put names to what they are experiencing and practice asking for what they need. (As adults, we need to be aware of when kids are communicating needs to us so that they learn that we respond and are there to help them!) Finally, using mindfulness and cognitive behavioral techniques, this book provides resources to help kids cope with negative feelings and thoughts safely and effectively.

In my psychology practice, I work with kids who have a hard time expressing their feelings every day. A common complaint I hear is, "Why do I feel this way? I don't have a reason to feel sad/angry/upset!" I like to say, "If feelings were logical, I would be out of a job." No feeling is inherently "good" or "bad," but some feelings are unpleasant and can seem irrational or even shameful. The activities in this book will help kids to not only understand and communicate their feelings, but it encourages them to develop a healthy relationship with their emotions, even when those emotions are unpleasant.

I can't promise no bad days, but I can help provide the tools to make those days bearable!

CONTENTS

A NOTE FROM THE AUTHOR

Children are constantly learning from their environment, and a key component in changing a child's behavior is identifying how the environment can support that change. That's why the first part of this book focuses on activities to support parents as they help their kids.

When working on self-regulation, I like to share with my clients and their parents some information about how our brains work. The amygdala, the part of our brain that experiences emotion, is fully developed when we are born. That means that even newborn babies experience grown up-sized feelings! But the frontal lobe, the part of our brain that processes language, controls impulses, and uses logic, keeps growing into adulthood. So, children and adolescents feel their emotions in the same way that adults do, but their brains have not yet developed the ability to process, communicate, or regulate these feelings the way that adults have.

On top of that, brain scan studies have shown that blood flow and activation in the frontal lobe goes down when the amygdala is activated, even in adults with fully developed brains. Have you ever said something in anger that you didn't mean? Or have you noticed how difficult it is to string together a coherent sentence when you're crying? That is because your amygdala is literally cutting off power to your frontal lobe.

The amygdala does not like to give up control without a fight. What is a typical reaction when someone is told to "calm down"? They get even more upset. If this is true for adults with full-grown brains, imagine how intense it is for children! In addition to this, no kid wants to feel reprimanded or get into trouble (attention-seeking behaviors aside). That's why we, the adults, need to approach moments when kids are escalated with compassion and from a teaching standpoint rather than a punitive one.

Parents: what do you mean if you say your child is "being bad"? It can be challenging to put words to exactly what "bad" means, but you know it when you see it. Kids conceptualize "being bad" in a similar way—when I ask a child in my office what gets them into trouble, they often reply, "When I'm bad," but when asked for specific examples, they get stuck. You need to specifically articulate *what* the behavior is that you have a problem with and present appropriate alternatives. This not only teaches your child what behaviors are acceptable, but specifying behaviors communicates the important distinction between a poor choice and a "bad kid."

Obviously, you love and care for your child. Otherwise, you would not be taking the time to read this and learn these skills. At the same time, you are probably feeling frustrated with the behaviors your child has when they are escalated. But if your child gets the message that they are bad, it not only decimates the child's self-esteem, but it can cause them to feel helpless to change. That helplessness can lead to more problem behaviors—after all, why should I bother trying to be better if I believe I'm incapable of making better choices?

First of all, a child should never, ever be reprimanded or punished for having a feeling. Feelings are okay! We all have them. It's okay to be angry, frustrated, sad, scared, or any other emotion! However, if we choose a problematic behavior while we are feeling a certain way, that can cause a problem. Parents can become overwhelmed, with their emotions feeding off of the child's emotions and causing tension to rise rather than fall. When your child has developed a habit of acting out in a negative way when they are escalated, it becomes tempting to respond preemptively to the feeling rather than the behavior. That is something that you, the parent, need to be mindful of.

Because kids are still learning about their emotions and understanding the connection between feelings, choices, and consequences, we need to approach difficult moments as teaching opportunities rather than as punishments. Children can get defensive if they think they are getting into trouble, so making these moments teachable starts with the parents. This section is written to the parent or guardian to help them respond in a way that supports the child's growth.

How Do I Respond To My Child's Emotions?

1. Although escalation can happen quickly, there is always a period between calm and explosion. What are my child's indicators that they are starting to have a problem? What changes in their voice, posture, movement, et cetera?

____

____

____

____

____

2. When I notice my child is escalating, what happens in my own body? What feelings or tensions arise for me, and how do I handle them?

____

____

____

____

3. How do I interact with my child in these moments? Do I speak with a harsh voice or a clam one? Do I threaten consequences or offer support?

____

____

____

____

____

4. How do I regulate my own feelings so that I can meet my child from a teaching perspective rather than a punishment perspective? How can I cue them to their own coping skills using both verbal and nonverbal communication that de-escalates rather than feeding into the situation?

____

____

____

____

Self-Care: Parents Need It Too!

There is an expression, "You can't pour from an empty glass." This means that you cannot help others if you are on empty yourself. To be the best parent you can be, you have to ensure that your own needs are also being met. This not only gives you the energy to be at your best for your kids, but it models for your children how to use coping skills in a healthy way. Children learn the most from their parents, and this learning is about 20% telling and 80% showing.

The next page will help you create your own self-care list that refills your glass.

What Fills Me Up?

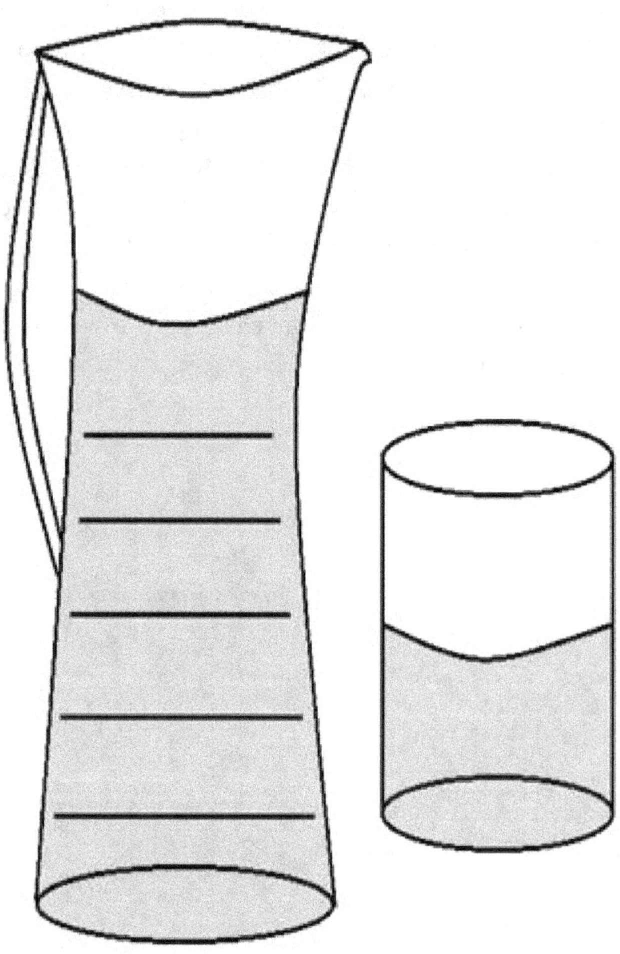

In the pitcher above, list activities that leave you feeling more "full," or feeling like you have more emotional resources, after you have done them. What rejuvenates you or makes you feel more able to share love with those around you?

PARENTING WITH YOUR PARTNER

This next activity is appropriate for parents, step-parents, foster parents, legal guardians, or anyone who finds themselves in the role of co-parenting a child. The goal is to open up communication between the co-parents, whether they are married, partnered, or separated.

It is important to remember that this is just a starting point. If you find that you and your co-parent(s) disagree about discipline, values, or parenting roles, you might need to look into co-parenting work to get on the same page.

For now, have each parent or guardian complete the activity on the next page to start this conversation. Remember that there are not "right" or "wrong" answers here; your answers should reflect what is true for you.

Mental health professionals: If completing this activity as a component of therapy, I recommend giving each parent this worksheet at the start of a session *when the child is not present* and review the results in the appointment together. This will help inform family treatment and possible recommendations for couple's counseling or co-parenting work outside of the child's sessions. It is also an excellent way to start conversations about parenting. Does one parent feel like they are always the "bad guy"? Do the parents disagree about what discipline is supposed to look like? Do they have vastly different perceptions of how parent-child interactions go in the home? This short quiz will help get everyone on the same page.

Co-Parenting Quiz

1. In co-parenting situations, what percent of the time am I
   in the role of (total should equal 100%):
   A. "Good Cop" ____________
   B. "Bad Cop" ____________
   C. United Front ____________
2. In co-parenting situations, what percent of the time do I
   think I should be in the role of (total should equal 100%):
   A. "Good Cop" ____________
   B. "Bad Cop" ____________
   C. United Front ____________
3. I feel like I need to "protect" my child from the other
   parent, either by withholding information about my
   child's behavior or shielding my child from my partner's
   emotions.
   A. Never
   B. On Occasion
   C. Sometimes
   D. Often
   E. Almost Always
4. When disciplining my child, it is most important to:
   A. Show the child why the behavior was wrong
   B. Punish the misbehavior
   C. Teach the child alternative choices
   D. Understand why the child acted out
5. I feel supported by my child's other parent.
   A. Never
   B. On Occasion
   C. Sometimes
   D. Often
   E. Almost Always

Talking To Children About Emotions

As adults, we often forget that we once had to learn about our feelings. We were not born knowing what different emotions feel like, or why certain feelings elicit different behaviors.

It is important to understand where your child is coming from when they are emotionally escalated so that you can teach them these skills. You can't communicate something if you do not have the right language and vocabulary to express it—that is why babies cry instead of asking politely to be changed. A child might have learned to speak but still lack the emotional language to express their feelings in a healthy way.

This workbook introduces different ways to teach these communication skills. To start, I want to provide you with some basic tools to take with you as you go through the rest of the book.

First, I have provided a feelings thermometer that allows your child to communicate how intense a feeling is using a scale of 1-10 to simplify putting that information into words. I encourage kids to try and put a word to the feeling as well as a number, but even something as simple as, "I feel bad, and it's at a seven," can be helpful in starting the conversation and allowing you to cue them to use an appropriate coping skill. This works best if the method is incorporated into daily conversations. For example, a parent can say, "Work was tough today. I feel stressed at about a five out of ten." This teaches the child what a five out of ten might look like and normalizes the activity.

Next, I have provided a chart to track when your child has used different skills. I strongly encourage you to and your child to practice different coping skills when everyone is calm. This way, your child is more likely to remember it in the moment. You can track both "practice" exercises and times that your child used a skill to de-escalate in the chart on page 17. This will help your child learn which skills are most helpful to them in different situations.

How Strong Are My Feelings?

Sometimes, you might feel a feeling just a tiny bit, and other times you might feel it a lot. Think about how you are feeling right now, and name that feeling. Then, focus on how strong the feeling is in your body. Do you feel the feeling a little bit? Do you feel it a medium amount? Or do you feel it the strongest you have ever felt?

Using the thermometer, choose a number from 1-10 to describe how intense the feeling is. 1 would be not having the feeling at all, and 10 would be the strongest you have ever had that feeling. You can use this to measure any kind of emotion: mad, sad, scared, or even happy!

Feeling: _______________________________

Date/Time	Triggering Event or Practice	Feeling Name	Feeling Strength Before	Skill Used	Feeling Strength After

PUNISHING VERSUS TEACHING

It is a natural response to want to punish problem behaviors, but people tend not to learn better choices from punishment. Effective discipline has its own sub-genre in the parenting books category, so I will keep things relatively simple here. For the purposes of this workbook, we want to help your child learn effective, appropriate, and healthy ways to express their feelings rather than acting out or "being bad." So how do you discipline a child for misbehavior in a way that teaches them to act differently in the future?

I am not saying that parents should never punish their children. Consequences are an essential part of learning! I am suggesting that parents take a mindful approach to discipline. Children learn from consequences that are consistent and linked to the problem behavior. As you learn to articulate your reasoning behind the punishment, you can communicate this to your child and help them learn.

On the next page is a chart that will help you list problem behaviors that you want to change, consequences for that behavior, and the reason why that consequence fits that behavior. As you demonstrate this cause-and-effect relationship to your child, they will not only learn about their behavior, they will begin to understand the connection between action and consequence as separate from the connection between emotion and action. You can't get into trouble for feeling mad if you still make good choices while you have that feeling!

For mental health professionals: This activity can be sent home with the parent, but I find that it makes a great family therapy session. Kids are more likely to follow through with behavior plans when they have a hand in determining consequences and rewards, and it gives the parents a calm, de-escalated space to explain the connection between behavior and consequence to the child. It also shows which behaviors the child feels are most problematic and facilitates positive communication between the parent and child.

Behavior	Consequence	Reason for Consequence

Remembering To Love Your Child

Of course you love your child! No matter how angry you feel or how terribly they act out, you still love them fully and unconditionally. That goes without saying, right?

Wrong! Kids need to hear that you love them. They need to see it in your behavior towards them, your body language, your tone, and even the way you look at them. Countless times I have facilitated a family session where I said, "You know your parent loves you even when you're in trouble, right?" and the child just stared at me, confused.

Remember, this whole workbook is about teaching children about emotions. One thing that children do not automatically know is that, while our emotions are temporary, we can love someone unconditionally. Your job as the parent is to teach them that unconditional love.

It is extra difficult to communicate love to your child when they are having "bad behavior." Parents are human, too—you get angry, frustrated, and upset just like anyone else. That is why I put together a gratitude journal to help you stay focused on what you love about your child. You can complete it as often as you want, but I especially encourage you to do it on days when it's extra difficult to show your child how much you love them. I also encourage you to sit down and share your answers with your child.

A Parent's Gratitude Journal

Child's Name: ___________________________

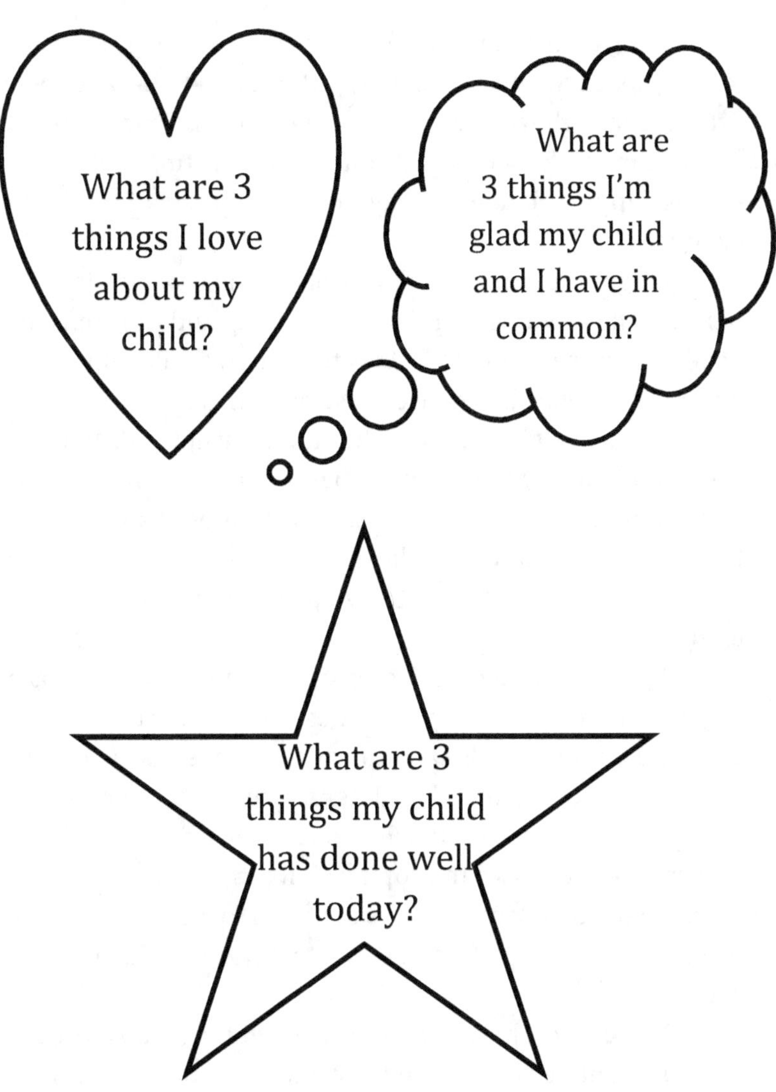

PART II: LET'S RELAX!

NOTE FROM THE AUTHOR

Before children can start identifying feelings and talking about them appropriately, they need to be able to de-escalate enough to even work on these skills. That is why, when I am working with kids on communicating their feelings appropriately, I always start with relaxation exercises.

I highly recommend that professionals work with parents on the Punishing Versus Teaching and Appropriate Feedback sessions in the last section, as this will help the parents cue their kids to use these activities in a way that encourages healthy coping rather than causing kids to feel ashamed or angry that they are being corrected. It can also help to "prescribe" using relaxation activities at specific times during the day regardless of how the child is feeling to help them get in the habit of paying attention to their emotions.

The relaxation exercises presented in this chapter are intended to be quick, easy activities that anyone can do at any time. Professionals can introduce the exercise when the child is in a neutral mood for later use and then work with parents to cue the activity when needed, with the goal being that the child chooses the coping skill rather than a problematic behavior. This means that I want you to notice when the child is starting to escalate, *before* a behavior has occurred.

The goal of these activities is to get the child's frontal lobe back online so they can be in a place to talk about their feelings appropriately. We want to get kids used to bringing down strong feelings in a healthy way so they can be in a place to learn more advanced skills.

Breathing

The following activities are created to help kids learn to take big, cleansing breaths. They take very little time and can be done anywhere.

It can help for parents to practice these activities with their kids to model the activities and normalize using the skill. This can also help the parent stay in control of their own emotions.

Relaxing breathing can de-escalate kids to the point that they can talk about their feelings appropriately and, hopefully, make a healthy rather than poor choice with that feeling.

Which breathing activity helps you the most?

Big Breath Activity

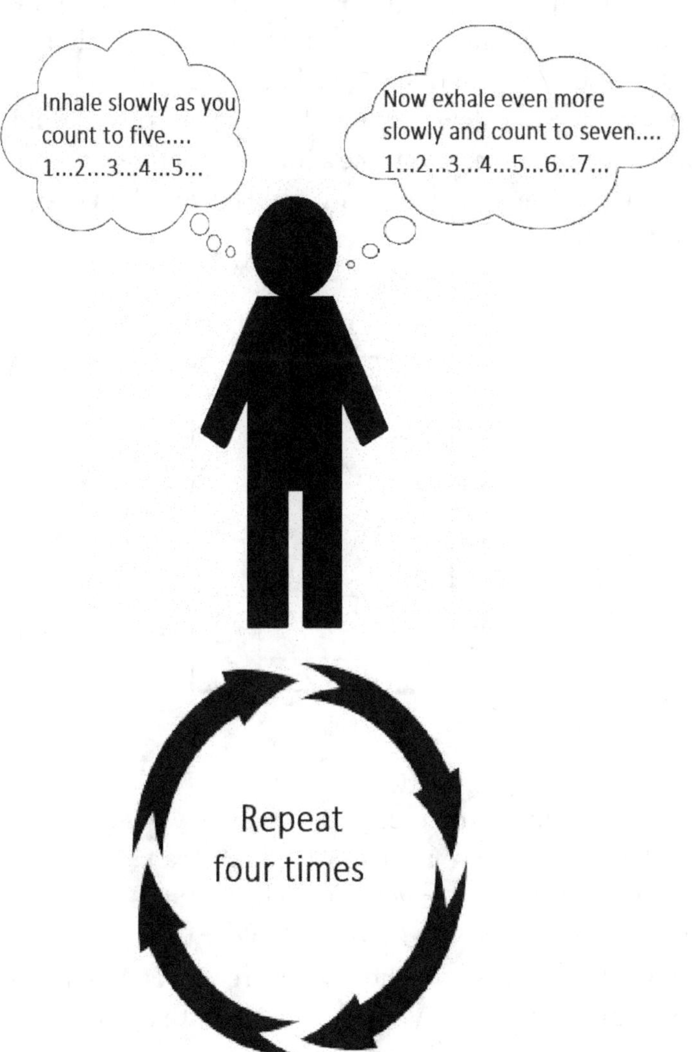

Square Breathing

This is an activity that you can do any time that you start to feel upset, angry, or sad. To start, use your pointer finger to trace a long line up as you take a big breath in. Then, hold your breath and trace a line horizontally in front of you. Next, breathe out slowly as you trace the line down. Hold your breath again as you trace a line back across to complete the square. Keep doing this until you feel your body become calm!

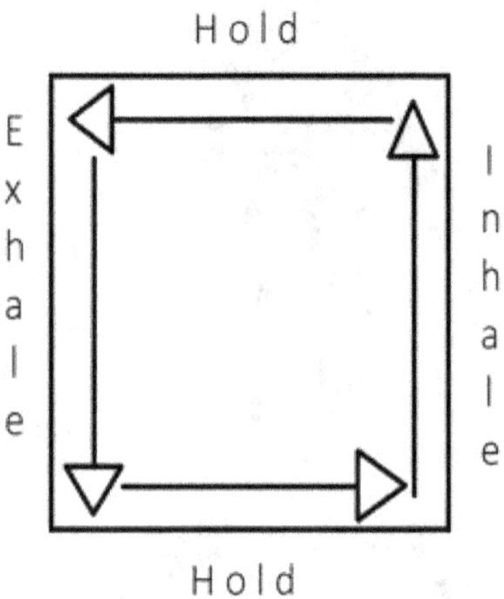

Each time you trace your square, try to go more slowly than the last time. If you'd like, you can say a four-word calming phrase as you make your square. One you can use is, "I am feeling calm." Slowly think or whisper, "I..." as you inhale, "Am..." as you hold your breath, "Feeling..." as you exhale, and "Calm..." as you hold your breath again.

Bubble Breathing

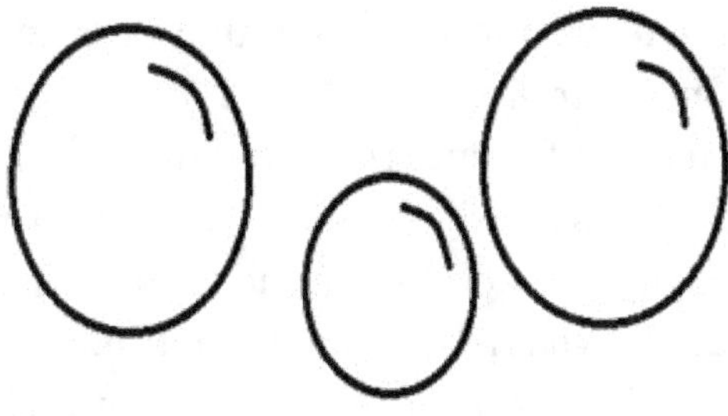

This activity will help you use your breath to let out unpleasant feelings.

When you want to bring a feeling down, take a big breath in through your nose. Fill your lungs and feel your belly get bigger with air. Imagine the air is a calm, happy feeling, and the more you breathe in, the more you are filled with that happy feeling.

Now, purse your lips and breathe out very slowly, like you are blowing a bubble. As you exhale, imagine that bubble filling with your emotion. Maybe the bubble is filling with anger, sadness, or fear. Picture the bubble getting bigger and bigger as you blow all the air out of your lungs.

When your lungs are empty, picture the bubble floating up, up, and away, taking the feeling with it and leaving you feeling clam.

Keep blowing bubbles until the negative feeling is gone, and you are left with the calm, happy feeling.

MUSCLE RELAXATION

We often tense our muscles without realizing it. Progressive muscle relaxation is a technique in which you deliberately tense different groups of muscles as tightly as you can before consciously relaxing them. This releases stress in the body and helps the mind relax. It also helps kids be more aware of what is going on in their bodies and notice their stress. On the next page is a script for muscle relaxation.

Relax Your Muscles

Sometimes when we feel stressed, we tense muscles we don't even think about. We can help these muscles feel relaxed by focusing on different muscle groups and consciously relaxing them.

Find a comfortable, seated position. You can go through the different muscle groups in your mind, or you can have someone read this to you. Take a few deep breaths to focus, and close your eyes. Imagine your muscles are sponges that have soaked up a bunch of water, and you have to squeeze all the water out.

Squeeze your toes and feet as tightly as you can, and picture water going down a drain. Count to five, then relax your feet completely.

Squeeze all the muscles in your legs as tightly as you can, and see the water swirling down the drain. Count to five as you squeeze, then relax your legs.

Do this again for your stomach muscles. Squeeze all the water out for five seconds, then relax.

Next, squeeze all the muscles in your hands and arms, and picture the water swirling down the drain. Count to five, then relax.

Last, squeeze the muscles in your shoulders, neck, and head. Count to five, picture the water running out, and relax your entire body completely.

You can do this any time you need to relax!

GROUNDING

Grounding refers to bringing yourself more fully into your body. This means that you become fully present in this moment rather than focusing on things that have already happened or might happen in the future. The reason it is important to remember to ground ourselves in this moment is that thinking about the past and future too much can cause strong, negative emotions that can become difficult to control. Grounding activities can help re-activate the "thinking part" of your brain, help you stay in control of your body, and make good choices. They serve to distract your child's mind from unpleasant emotions that might cause then to act out.

Grounding works by bringing attention either to sensations in the body or the environment around us. What works best depends on both individual preferences and the current environment. For example, people with pain issues often prefer activities that center their focus on external things rather than on the discomfort in their bodies, but someone trying to self-regulate in a stressful environment might prefer to look inward.

You can use the practice sheet in the first chapter of this manual to help your child determine which activities are most relaxing to them.

The Five Senses Game

 Sight: What are five things I can see?

 Sound: What are four things I can hear?

 Touch: What are three things I can feel?

 Smell: What are two things I can smell?

 Taste: What is one thing I can taste?

Looking Mindfully

When is the last time you looked really, really closely at something? So closely that you took in *all* the little details? Taking in the tiny details about an object can refocus your mind when you are having an unpleasant feeling. You can do this activity any time you want to relax. You can go through the steps in your own mind, or you can ask someone to read this to you while you do the activity.

First, find an object for this activity. I like to use a rock, seashell, leaf, or flower. Sit in a comfortable position, and hold the item in your open hand.

If you're comfortable, close your eyes, and start by taking a few big breaths, in to the count of five and out to the count of seven. You can use one of the breathing activities from Part II if you'd like.

When you feel your body relax, open your eyes, and look at the object in your hand. Look at it very closely, noticing its shape and edges, its colors and patterns. Try to list all the different colors you can see. Turn it slowly and see how it changes when you look at it from different angles. Feel its weight in your hand—how heavy is it? What kind of texture does it have? Do parts of it feel different than others? How big is it?

When you think you've seen every detail there is, look a little bit longer. What do you see that you didn't notice at first?

How did it feel to look at something this closely? As you go about your day, see what else you notice about things you might look at all the time!

The Categories Game

This game can be played anywhere and with just about anything, on your own or with a friend. Your task is to choose a category and then name at least five things that fit into that category. For example, if you choose "colors," you could say, "Orange, pink, teal, navy, and lavender." If you are playing with a friend, take turns thinking of things for that category and see who can go the longest wtihout getting stumped. Try to choose a category that is fun and relaxing to think about, but other than that, there are no rules!

Distractions

I'm sure at some time or another you've noticed that the world around you is full of distractions. Sometimes this is frustrating, like when you need to listen at school but there is a bird outside the window, or when your parent is asking you to do something but you would rather be playing video games. But when you are experiencing an unpleasant feeling distracting yourself is a great way to keep that feeling from becoming a bad behavior.

Below are some different distractions you can focus on when you want to let go of a feeling that you don't like. These are just examples—you can add your own, too!

What is your favorite color?

How many things can you see right now that have that color?

How many things near you are moving right now?

How many things are making a sound?

Are there people around you right now? Imagine each of them in a different Halloween costume!

How high can you count, going by 7s?

7... 14...? ? ?

Part III: What's Going On Inside My Body?

A Note from the Author

The first step in communicating feelings is learning to recognize when we feel them. Now that your child has some skills to de-escalate intense emotions, we can start to work on identifying what happens in the child's body when they experience these feelings. Because kids are not experienced in identifying emotions and using words to describe how they are feeling, they often do not even realize they are having a feeling or that the feeling needs to be communicated until they are bursting with it!

The thermometer from the first chapter illustrates this point. For many children, by the time they decide to share with the parent that they feel angry, the emotion might be at an 8/10. It can be very difficult to come down from 8/10 without an outburst, and it is difficult to communicate appropriately when an emotion is that high. We want the child to notice what anger feels like when it is lower, say at 4/10 instead.

The activities in this chapter help kids tune in to their bodies to notice when they are escalating and what might be setting off the escalation. We want them to get in tune with what is happening on the inside, so that we can help them communicate what they are feeling and so they can learn to regulate those feelings appropriately.

Coloring Our Feelings

I have talked a bit about how the feelings part of our brain can make it difficult to use the talking part of our brain. For these next few activities, kids can use colors to express your emotions rather than words. If they would like, they can name the colors with feelings words.

Parents might want to incorporate this activity into daily conversation, asking questions like, "What color do you feel right now?" instead of trying to get the child to use specific feelings words that they are still learning to understand.

Color Your Emotions

What Color Is Your Feeling?

Do you feel red or yellow?
Maybe you feel green or purple?
Do you feel black or gray today?

Where In Your Body Do You Feel It?

Is the feeling in your stomach or your chest?
Do you feel it in your head?
Maybe you feel it in your hands or feet?

What Kind Of Feeling Is It?

Is the feeling pleasant or unpleasant?
When have you felt this way before?
Do you need help bringing this feeling down?

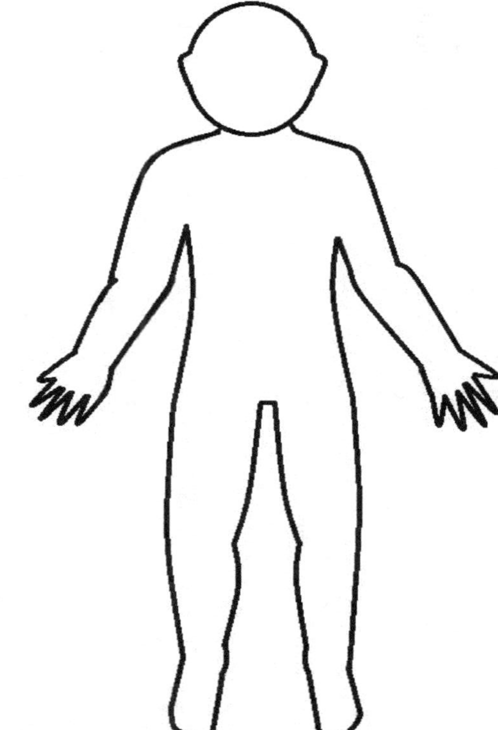

What Does My Feeling Look Like?

Draw your feeling in the space below. What colors does it have? Does it have a shape? Does it look like something you've seen before? Does it have a lot of dark lines or quick scribbles? Use this page to show what your feeling looks like.

Learning About Body Sensations

In this section, we will learn about different sensations that happen in different parts of our bodies. Some sensations might be more pleasant than others, but none of them are automatically "good" or "bad." A lot of body sensations can feel positive in one situation but negative in another.

First, we will learn about what different sensations or feelings can feel like in our bodies. Then, we will explore what kinds of situations these sensations are linked to, and when they might feel pleasant or unpleasant.

This will prepare us for the next chapter, which will help us put names to the many, many feelings we experience.

What Sensations Does My Body Experience?

Below are different sensations you might feel in your body. Think about times when you have felt these things. Did you like the sensation? What was going on right before you felt that way? What did the sensation make you want to do? What other body sensations can you think of?

What Other Sensations Does My Body Experience?

What else do you feel in your body sometimes? Aside from the ones listed on the last page, draw or write some other body sensations you've noticed below.

When Do I Feel Different Sensations?

When is a time that I felt dizzy? _______________________________

When is a time I cried? _______________________________

When is a time I felt my eyes go wide? _______________________________

When is a time I had a headache? _______________________________

When is a time I felt my heart race? _______________________________

When is a time my hands felt shaky? _______________________________

When is a time my mouth felt dry? _______________________________

When is a time I was sweaty? _______________________________

When is a time my stomach hurt? _______________________________

When is a time I shivered? _______________________________

When is a time my breathing was fast? _______________________________

When is a time my muscles were tense? _______________________________

What about the sensations I came up with? _______________________________

____

____

I Can Change How My Body Feels

Sometimes, we have sensations in our bodies because we are experiencing an emotion (like feeling warm when we are angry or crying when we are sad). Other times, something in our environment gives us a sensation (like shivering when we feel cold). But sometimes, we can change our body sensations!

For this activity, you will need a timer and your favorite breathing activity from the second part of this book. Find your heartbeat on your chest, wrist, or neck. Use the timer (or ask an adult to help you) and time your pulse for 10 seconds. What was your pulse? _________

Next, do jumping jacks or run in place for 30 seconds. Go as fast as you can! At the end of 30 seconds, take your pulse for 30 seconds again: _________

Now, sit or lay in a comfortable position on a couch or on the floor. Stretch a little bit to relax your body, and take a big breath in through your nose, then let the breath out through your mouth. Try to breathe as slowly as you can. After you've taken five slow, deep breaths, take your pulse for the third time: _________

See how your body responded to your behavior? When you became really active, your heart beat faster, and when you relaxed, it slowed down! Even though we don't choose how we are feeling, we can make choices that can affect what's going on inside our bodies.

What other ways can you affect what's happening in your body?

Part IV: Name Your Feelings!

A Note From The Author

Now that we have developed some relaxation tools and helped kids learn to cue into what is going on inside of their bodies, we are ready to take the next step: communicating this information to others. The activities in this chapter are aimed at teaching kids vocabulary about their feelings, connecting those terms to body sensations and emotions, and identify times when they might be experiencing more than one feeling at a time.

By the end of this chapter, your child should have the language to express their feelings with words!

How Can I Identify Feelings?

In this section, we will work on naming different feelings and identifying what they look and feel like. Many feeling names are provided, but feel free to add as many as you can think of!

After we have identified different feelings, we will look at how these feelings show up on people's faces and what they feel like in our bodies. You will notice what body sensations go with different feelings, which will help you identify what you are feeling sooner.

Don't worry about describing the "right" body sensations to go with different feelings—there are no "right" or "wrong" answers in this section. There is only what feels right to you!

Feeling Names: How Many Can You Think Of?

Happy

Sad

Angry

Scared

Surprised

Excited

Annoyed

Frustrated

Calm

Impatient

Tired

Hyper

Agitated

Exhausted

Terrified

Nervous

Relaxed

Furious

Rested

Upset

Tearful

Tense

How Do Feelings Show On My Face?

Now that we have named many different feelings, let's think about how those feelings show on our faces. Most people show emotion with different facial expressions. Below are some blank faces. Fill them in with how you show those feelings on your face.

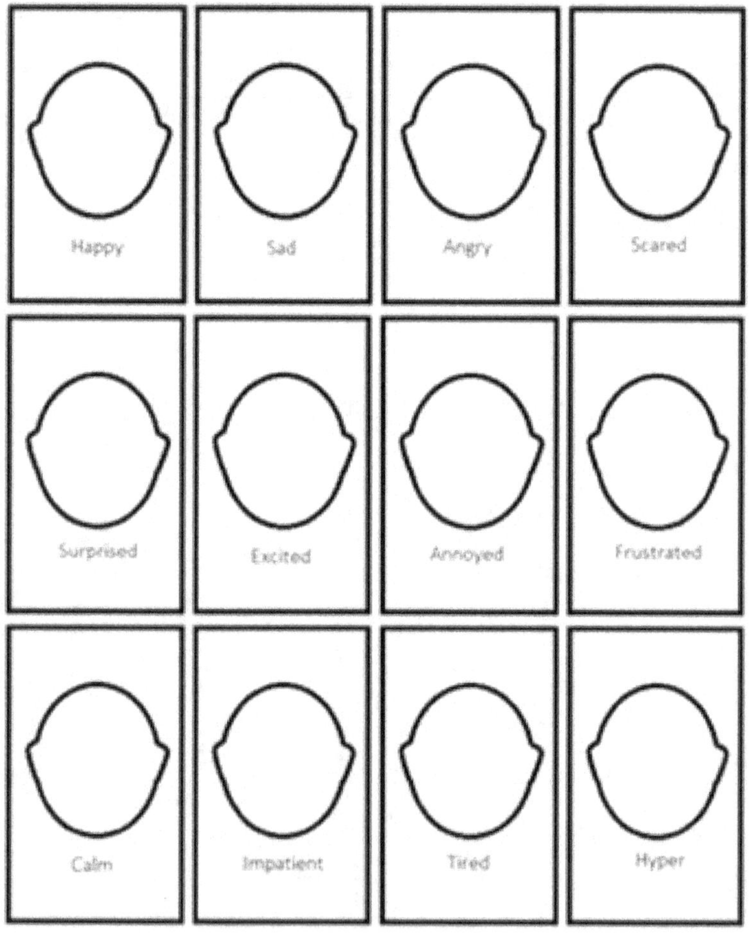

How Do Other Feelings Show On My Face?

Now you can choose more feelings and show how they look on your face!

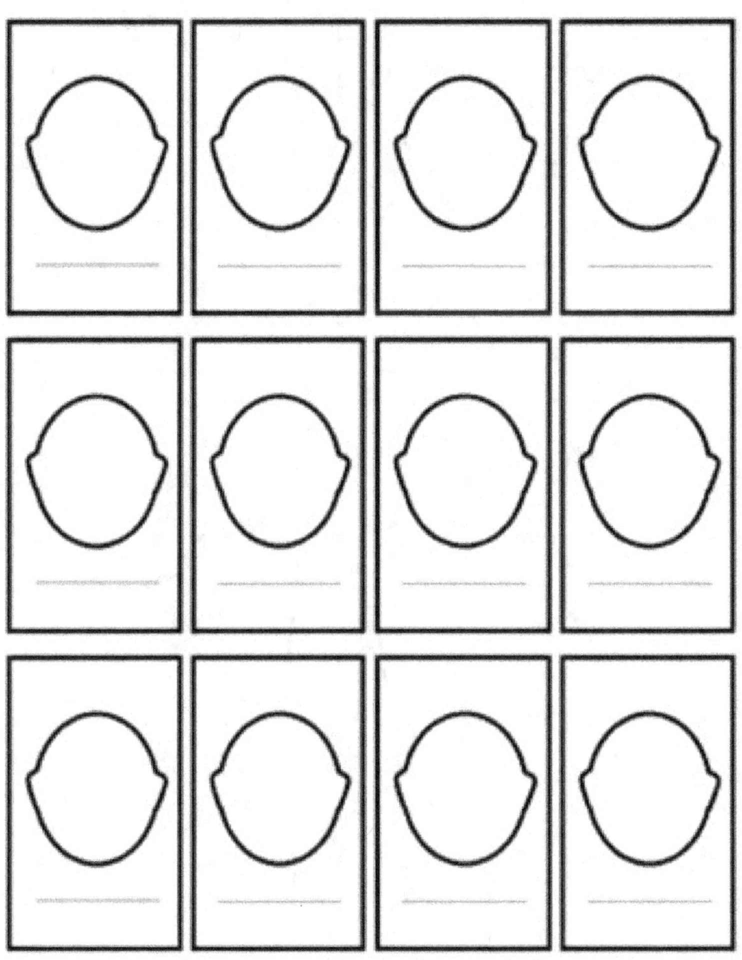

What Happens In My Body When I Feel Happy?

Think about a time that you felt really happy, at a 6/10 or more. On the body below, draw or write what sensations you felt. How does happy feel on your face? Your arms or shoulders? Your stomach? What about your legs and feet? How does happy feel different to you from other emotions?

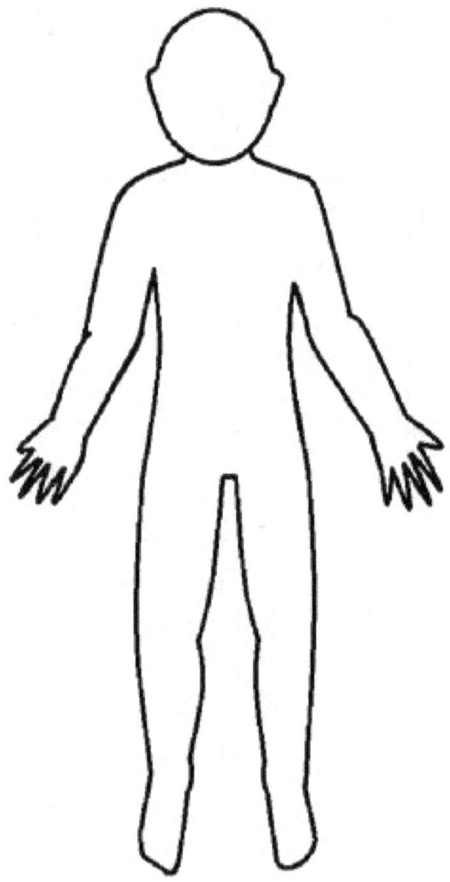

What Happens In My Body When I Feel Sad?

Think about a time that you felt really sad, at a 6/10 or more.
On the body below, draw or write what sensations you felt.
How does sad feel on your face? Your arms or shoulders?
Your stomach? What about your legs and feet? How does sad
feel different to you from other emotions?

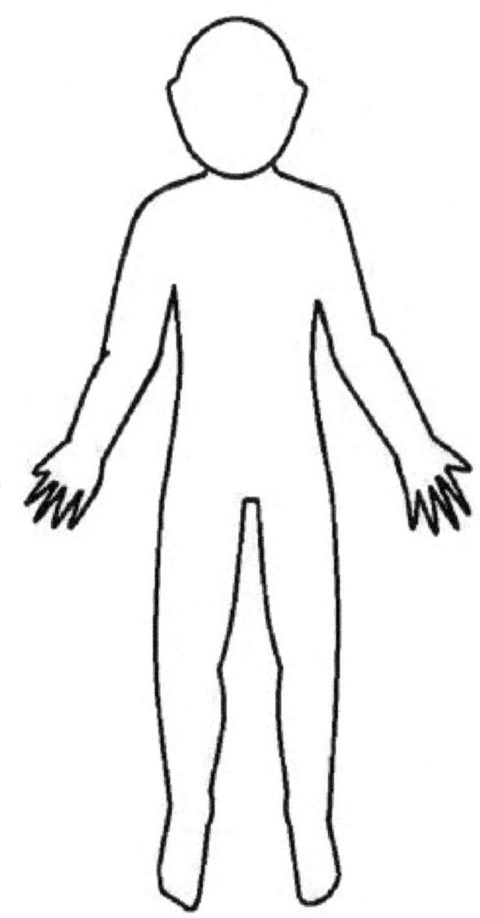

What Happens In My Body When I Feel Mad?

Think about a time that you felt really mad, at a 6/10 or more. On the body below, draw or write what sensations you felt. How does mad feel on your face? Your arms or shoulders? Your stomach? What about your legs and feet? How does mad feel different to you from other emotions?

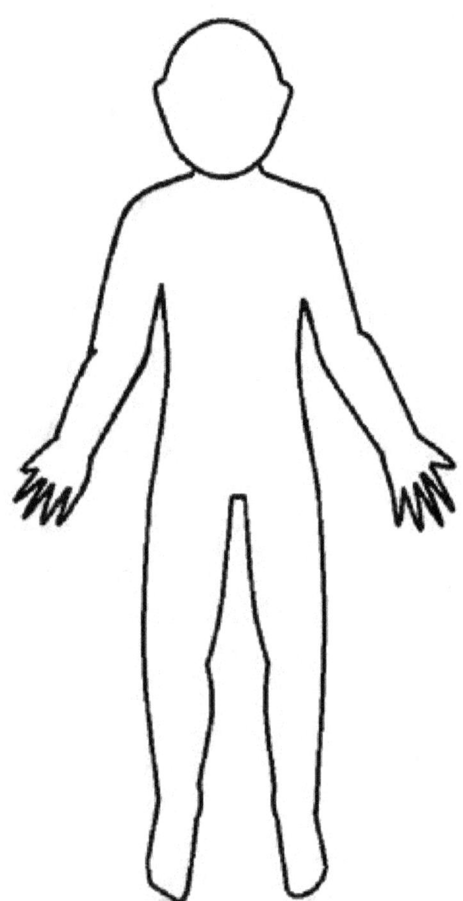

What Happens In My Body When I Feel Scared?

Think about a time that you felt really scared, at a 6/10 or more. On the body below, draw or write what sensations you felt. How does scared feel on your face? Your arms or shoulders? Your stomach? What about your legs and feet? How does scared feel different to you from other emotions?

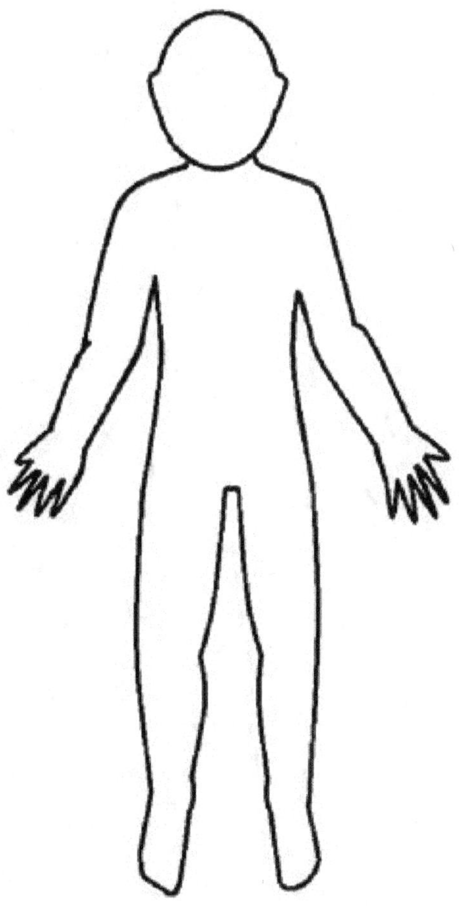

What Happens In My Body When I Feel ________?

Now it's your turn! Choose a feeling you haven't done yet and draw how it feels in your body like you did with the other feelings. You might choose a feeling that you really enjoy having or a feeling that is hard to deal with. Think about a time you were at a 6/10 or more of that feeling and draw or write what sensations you felt.

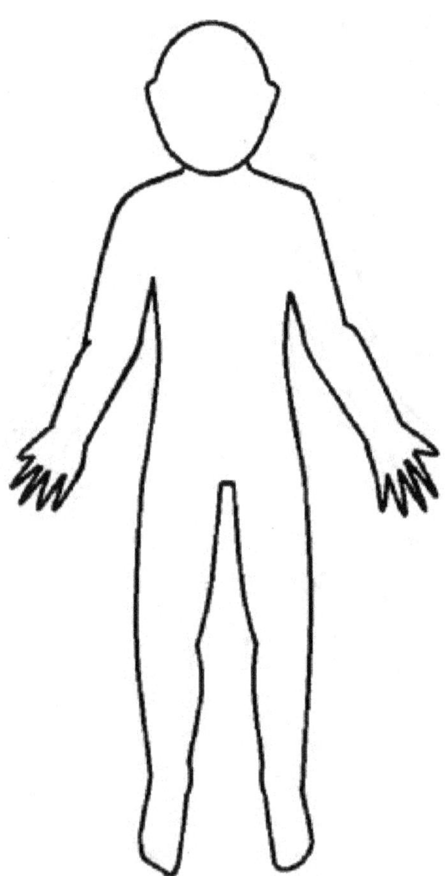

WHAT CAUSES FEELINGS?

A feeling by itself is not good or bad, though it can be unpleasant. We do not get into trouble when we feel angry, but we will probably get into trouble if we hurt someone out of anger. We are still responsible for our behavior regardless of how we feel—if we knock over a vase and break it in our excitement, there will probably be consequences even though most people enjoy feeling excited.

So far in this chapter, we have worked on knowing names for feelings and recognizing them in our bodies. Now, we will talk about what sets off different feelings in us.

Feelings often do not make sense, and there is never a "right" or "wrong" way to feel. Something that one person finds exciting might scare someone else, or something that one person thinks is funny might cause someone else to feel sad.

These next few activities are designed to help kids identify what brings up different feelings for them, as well as recognizing more than one feeling at a time.

Different Things Make Me Feel Different Ways!

Some things might make us feel a little bit irritated, and other things might make us REALLY angry! Some things might make us a little happy, and something else might make us SO EXCITED! How strong are your feelings about different things? Fill in the thermometers below to show how big your feelings get about different things, and make up some of your own!

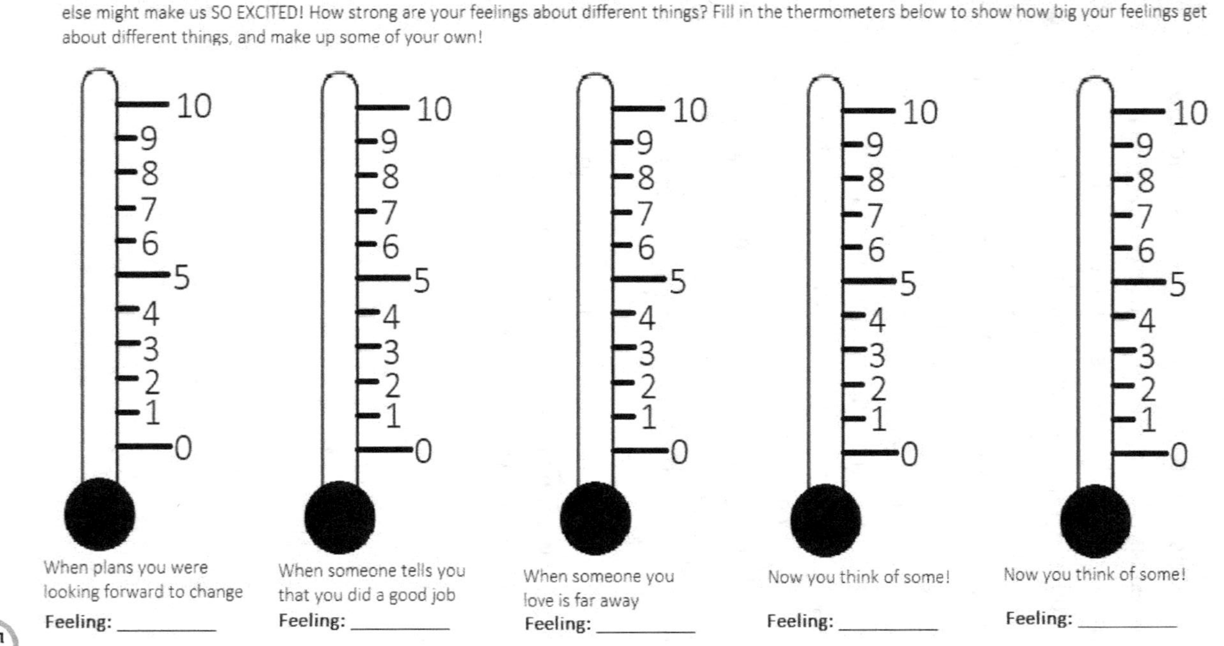

When plans you were looking forward to change

Feeling: _____________

When someone tells you that you did a good job

Feeling: _____________

When someone you love is far away

Feeling: _____________

Now you think of some!

Feeling: _____________

Now you think of some!

Feeling: _____________

When Have I Felt Different Things?

In the space below, draw or write about a time when you felt very, very happy. Think about a time when your happiness was at a 6/10 or higher on your feelings thermometer:

When Have I Felt Different Things?

Now, draw or write about a time when you felt extremely sad. Think about a time when you felt sadness at a 6/10 or higher on the feelings thermometer.

When Have I Felt Different Things?

On this page, write or draw about a time when you felt incredibly angry. Think of a time when your anger was at least 6/10 on the feelings thermometer, and share that time below:

When Have I Felt Different Things?

Next, write or draw about a time when you felt very scared or afraid, at a 6/10 or higher on the feelings thermometer:

When Have I Felt Different Things?

Now you choose! Pick a feeling we haven't already done, and write about a time when you felt it very strongly.

The feeling I chose is: _________________________

Two Feelings At Once??

Sometimes, something happens that brings up more than one feeling. These feelings might cause similar sensations in our bodies, like if you are on a roller coaster and feel butterflies in your stomach because you are both scared and excited at the same time. Other times, the feelings might seem completely opposite, and you might wonder how they can occur together at all, like if a friend gets something that you also wanted, and you feel happy for them but also jealous.

Below, draw what it feels like to have two feelings at once. You can pick any two feelings, or choose a time that you felt two ways about something.

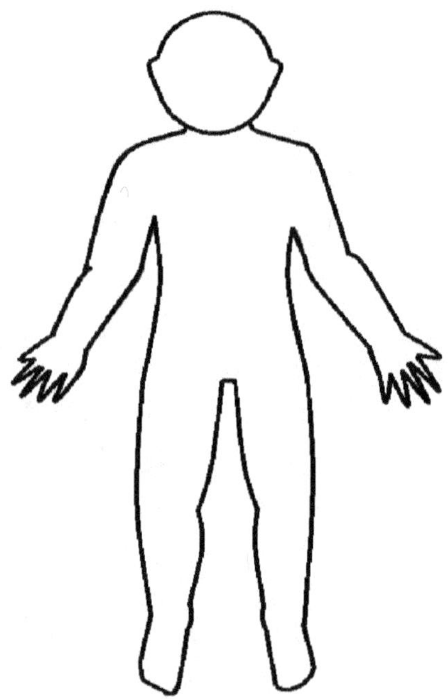

Part V: Asking For Help (Relationships)

A Note From The Author

In the first chapter, we talked about taking a teaching-oriented approach rather than a punishment approach to "bad" behaviors. The teaching approach helps kids learn how to make better choices in the future because they learn appropriate alternatives rather than just learning what behaviors lead to punishment. In this same vein, we want to create a space for kids to ask for and receive help when they need it without choosing a bad behavior. The activities in this section will help children identify who can help them when they are having trouble with their emotions.

Now that we have introduced the vocabulary for kids to name their emotions and helped them connect those emotions to specific body sensations, we want to show them how to use this new skill effectively. Because children's brains are still developing, they often physically lack the capacity to self-regulate on their own, and they often need support from the adults who love them to de-escalate successfully and safely.

Although this chapter still focuses on teaching communication skills to the child, parents should also actively participate. It does a child no good if they communicate a need, and the parent does not understand what they are communicating or does not respond in a way that is helpful.

Kids and their parents need to be speaking the same language when it comes to emotions. This means not only that they need to be using the same words, but also be on the same page about acceptable ways to use these words to get help. If, for example, your child becomes escalated in the grocery store and attempts to tell you that they need to step outside, telling them they need to wait or "hold it together" is not helping them de-escalate. In fact, in that moment, you are teaching your child that asking for help is not an effective way to get their need met, and so they are not only less likely to try communicating with words in the future, but they are just as close to a "meltdown" or "tantrum" as they were before they asked you for help!

We want kids to know that it is okay and appropriate to ask for help. We want kids to be able to identify whom they can go to when they need help, and we need those adults to be receptive and helpful when this happens.

Finally, we want to create a language based on the child's developmental level and ability so that they can tell you what their needs are. Sometimes a parent will want the child to say, "May I please take a break," which is a very nice way to ask. But if a five-year-old is at an 8/10 angry, they might not have enough frontal lobe activity in the moment to put that sentence together! This chapter is about communicating needs and managing parent expectations for what this communication might look like.

WHO HELPS ME?

Everyone needs help sometimes! Below are different situations to get you thinking about who you can ask for help when you need it. For each, think about whom you would ask for help if you were in that situation.

1. When I don't understand an assignment at school.

   ____

2. When another kid is saying mean things that hurt my feelings.

   ____

3. When I trip and get a scrape on my knee.

   ____

4. When I feel very sad and I don't know why.

   ____

5. When I'm feeling so angry that I want to break something.

   ____

6. When I miss someone who lives very far away.

   ____

7. When I feel like I am going to throw up.

____

8. When I break something by accident.

____

9. When I do something that hurts someone else.

____

10. When I am so excited that I don't know if I can control my body.

____

When are some other times that you might need to ask for help? And who helps you when these things happen?

11. ___________________________________

____

12. ___________________________________

____

13. ___________________________________

____

How Do I Know I Need Help?

Every single person in the world needs help sometimes: you, your friends, siblings, parents, and even teachers need help with things sometimes. It is okay to need help, and it is okay to ask for help when you need it. You should not get into trouble for asking for help. Everyone has trouble making the right choices sometimes, and everyone sometimes has strong feelings that are difficult to control. When this happens, we want people to be able to ask for and receive the help they need!

But in order to ask for help, you need to recognize that you need it. How do you know that you are starting to have trouble? Use the body below to draw or label the body sensations, feeling words, thoughts, or even situations that might make it difficult for you to make good choices. This will help you notice when you need to ask for help!

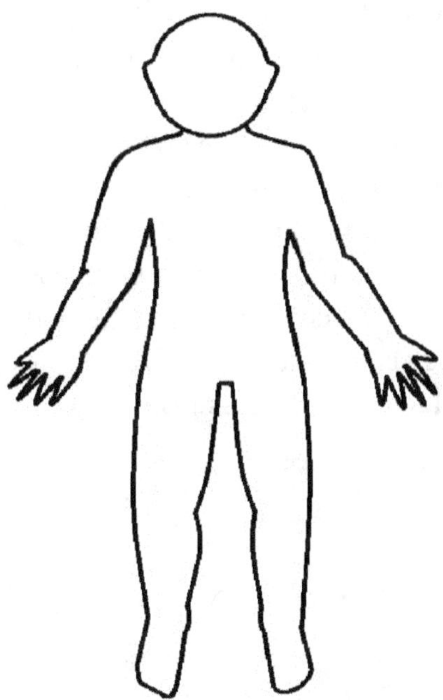

ASKING FOR AND RECEIVING HELP

Now that we have reviewed identifying when to ask for help, we can determine what asking for and receiving help looks like. Kids communicate through behavior, and so a child who is "being bad" is often trying to communicate in a way that the parent does not understand. We want to teach them the appropriate and effective ways to ask for help.

At the same time, though, we want to make sure that the tools we are teaching kids will be accessible in moments when they are emotionally escalated. We want to manage parents' expectations and give kids a method of asking for help that is appropriate but also possible when they feel angry or upset. These activities will help families develop a method of communication that works for everyone involved.

We also want kids to learn how to receive help when they need it. Have you ever noticed that the most effective way to make someone escalate further is to ask them to "calm down"? There will be times when your child does not have the insight to notice that they need help with their emotions, so parents will need to prompt them to receive help and de-escalate, and parents need to cue them in a way that will not cause the child to become defensive. Kids, in turn, need to be able to accept help when it is offered. This next section addresses these issues.

My Ask-For-Help Plan

Who are the adults I can ask for help? _______________________

____

Sometimes, when we are having a hard time with our emotions, it's hard to use words to share what we are feeling. That's why it can be good to have an ask-for-help plan. Make this plan with your parent or guardian, and share it with adults you trust so they understand the plan and can offer help when you need it.

If I need help with my
feelings, my code word is: _______________________

If I can't use words, I can cue
adults I trust by: _______________________

When I feel angry, the most
helpful thing adults can do is: _______________________

When I feel sad, the most
helpful thing adults can do is: _______________________

When I feel hyper, the most
helpful thing adults can do is: _______________________

When I feel __________, the
most helpful thing adults can _______________________
do is:

Adults Want To Help Me When I Need It!

Sometimes, it might be hard to ask for help with our feelings. We might not even realize we could use help when the feelings come up. One of the ways adults can support you is by noticing when you might need help and offer it before you ask. It can be hard for kids to accept help, and sometimes kids feel mad or frustrated that the adult has noticed they are having a hard time. We want to prepare you to be able to accept help when you need it.

When my parent notices that I am having a hard time with my feelings and wants to help me, they can let me know!

1. They will take me aside, one-on-one, to let me know they noticed I'm having a hard time so I don't feel embarrassed.
2. They will let me know specifically what they noticed I'm struggling with. Am I being loud or disruptive? Am I having a hard time controlling my body? Am I doing something that could hurt myself, someone else, or break something?
3. They will give me two coping or relaxation skills to choose from that might help me. I can suggest another skill if I want, and my parent will tell me if it's an option right now.
4. We will do the coping skill **together**, and I will use my words (if I can) to tell them what I feel in my body while we do the skill.
5. They will remind me that they love and care about me!

Adults Want To Help Me When I Need It!

When my parent notices that I might need help with my choices, I will remember:

1. That it is okay to ask for and receive help from adults! It's their job to help me when I need it, and it's my job to listen to them when they try to help me.
2. That I am **not in trouble** for needing help. My parent is offering me help **before** I make a choice that might get me into trouble.
3. That it is okay to have a hard time, a bad day, and to make mistakes. Everyone, including my parent, makes mistakes sometimes.
4. That I can get back to my day as soon as I am in control of my body and making good choices.
5. That my parent loves me so much! They are trying to help me make good choices and learn how to handle my feelings appropriately because they care so much about me.

PART VI: COPING SKILLS!

A NOTE FROM THE AUTHOR

We have talked about how feelings operate. We have learned how to take a teaching approach rather than punishment when your child misbehaves. We have developed relaxation skills as well as communication skills to name and share our feelings. We have learned about asking for and receiving help when we need it.

Now, in this last chapter, we will help your child create their very own toolbox of coping skills. This toolbox will include the relaxation exercises from the second chapter of this workbook, as well as more in-depth coping skills. It is recommended that kids try out many different skills to notice which ones work best for them, and they might find that what helps them when they are angry is not helpful when they are sad.

By the end of this chapter, children should have a list of coping skills that they personally find helpful. You can get a folder or small binder and put together a packet of the skills that worked for them so that they don't have to remember each one. When they are having trouble, the parent can direct the child to the coping skills packet to cue them to use these skills appropriately.

LISTENING (AND RESPONDING) TO MY BODY

The skills in this section are based on mindfulness. "Mindfulness" means bringing our attention to the present moment and becoming fully aware of what is happening right now. This builds on some of the grounding techniques from before. We want to teach kids to use their awareness of body sensations to cope with uncomfortable or unpleasant feelings.

My Heart Is Racing!

Big feelings have a big effect on our bodies. One thing most kids notice when they have a big feeling is their heart beats faster. When our hearts beat faster, the blood travels to all our muscles and makes us ready to move. So let's put that blood to work!

When you notice your heart start to beat faster, ask a parent or someone you trust to get a timer, and see how many jumping jacks you can do in one minute! If you don't like jumping jacks, you can choose another exercise you like better.

After one minute is up, put your hand over your chest and feel how fast your heart is beating now. Take a deep breath, and notice if the feeling changes. You just gave that energy somewhere to go instead of having it bottle up inside you!

Shock Your Senses!

When you feel "stuck" in a big feeling, sometimes it can help to experience a very strong sensation to snap you out of it. This activity can help you get un-stuck.

Take a piece of ice from your freezer, and hold it to a part of your body where you can feel your pulse (your wrist or neck are good spots for this). Feel how cold it is! Try and keep the ice cube in one place while you slowly count to five. The cold sensation will distract your brain from the feeling.

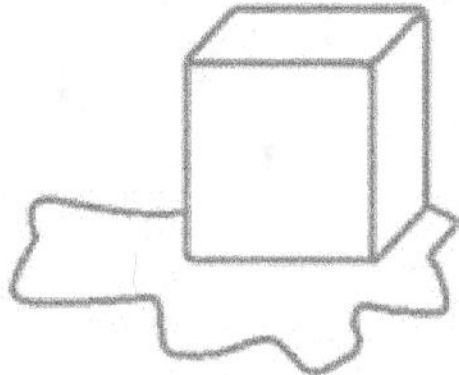

Ask your parent if you have vanilla extract in your house. (Perfume or essential oil can work for this too!) Close your eyes and hold the open container under your nose. Take a big sniff. What do you smell? How do you feel? (Make sure pets are not in the room while you do this, as they can be extra sensitive to smells, and essential oils can make them sick!)

Take a breath mint or piece of hard candy with a strong flavor. (Spearmint or peppermint work really well for this, but you can choose another flavor that you like.) Place it on your tongue and close your mouth. Feel the taste of the mint in your mouth and in your nose. How does it taste? If you'd like, try biting into the mint. How did it feel? Did it change the flavor?

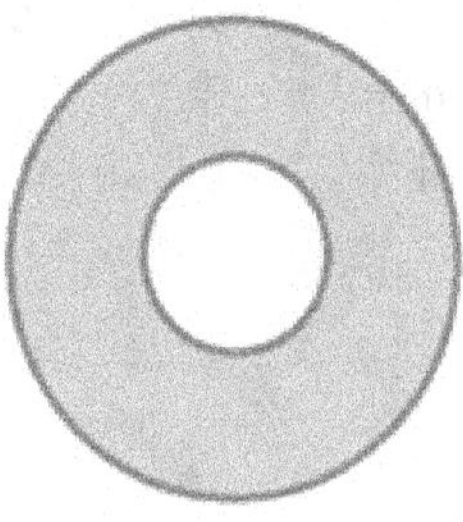

Sometimes I Just Want To Squish Something!!

Sometimes when you feel mad or sad, you might feel like smashing things! It can feel good to squish something, but you want to choose something that won't break or get you into trouble. You can buy putty at the store, or you can make slime or play dough with help from an adult. Play around with different kinds to find a texture that you really like, and you can squish something any time you need to!

Parents: please be aware that these activities can be messy, so put newspaper down before making these recipes. Make sure to store what you make in sealed containers so it lasts longer, and when playing with the product, use a hard surface, as slime can stain carpet.

Slime Recipe
COMBINE

White glue (1 cup)

Baking soda (1/2 tsp)

Water (1/3 cup)

Boric acid (contact solution) (1-3/4 tbsp)

OPTIONAL

Shaving cream (adds fluff)

Food coloring (adds color)

Glitter (adds sparkle)

Foam beads (adds crunch)

IF SLIME IS TOO

Sticky – add more baking soda

Watery – add more boric acid

Stiff – add more water

Play Dough Recipe
Warm water (2 cups)
Vegetable oil (2 tbsp)
Flour (2 cups)
Salt (1 cup)

Mix water and oil together.
Mix flour and salt together.

Once combined,
mix both together
and knead like bread
until smooth.

IF PLAY DOUGH IS TOO
Sticky – add flour
Watery – add flour
Flaky – add water

Silly Putty Recipe
COMBINE
Liquid starch (1/2 cup)
White glue (1 cup)
Food coloring (if desired to add color)

IF PUTTY IS TOO
Sticky – add starch
Flaky – add glue

Visualization Activities

Visualization activities involve picturing calming or relaxing scenarios to bring down anxiety, anger, or other feelings. By helping the child come up with specific visualizations when they are calm, you give them a tool that they can use any time, anywhere, that they need help de-escalating.

Before introducing visualization activities, you want to make sure that the child is capable of visualization. A lot of people do not realize that one to three percent of us actually cannot picture images in our minds! This is called aphantasia. People with aphantasia can still benefit from guided meditations, but they might find the guided visualization aspect confusing or frustrating.

Choose a shape and color (for example, a blue square), and ask the child to picture it in their mind. Ask them to describe what they "see." This will allow the child to articulate how strongly they are able to visualize and will tell you whether guided visualization activities are a good fit for them.

Your Calm Place

If you feel comfortable, close your eyes and picture a place where you feel very calm and in control of your body. This place can be somewhere real or somewhere that you made up in your mind. Below, please draw or write about this place, using as many details as you can think of. Include what you can see, hear, feel, smell, and taste. Is someone with you, or are you alone? What are you doing? How do you feel, and what's going on inside your body?

You can imagine you are in your calm place any time you feel angry, sad, or anxious!

Changing The Radio Station

Unpleasant thoughts or bad memories sometimes come into our heads without us wanting them to. These thoughts can be untrue or just unhelpful, and memories can make us feel like a terrible thing is happening all over again even if we are safe right now. But if we just tell the thought to go away, it can seem like it sticks around even more!

Imagine that your brain is a radio, like the one in the car or an old boom box. Your thoughts are the radio station that is playing. Sometimes, you choose what is playing on the radio, like putting in a CD that you like. But other times, you are listening to whatever the DJ chooses to play on that station. When the DJ is choosing the songs, sometimes they might put on a song that you really like, and you want to get up and dance! Other times, the DJ might be talking about something that is boring to you, and you might listen without really hearing what is being said. But other times, a song might come on that you just HATE and do not want to listen to. When you are having thoughts or memories you do not like, it's as if that horrible song is playing on repeat.

The good news is, you do not have to keep listening to the bad song! You can *change the station*. Pretend that your nose is the dial, and press or twist it to change your brain's radio station. If your parent notices that you seem to be listening to a bad song, they can press your nose to change the station for you.

Now, imagine that you have just tuned in to a new station. This station is playing your favorite song! What song is playing on the new station? Sing or hum that song to replace the bad thought or memory.

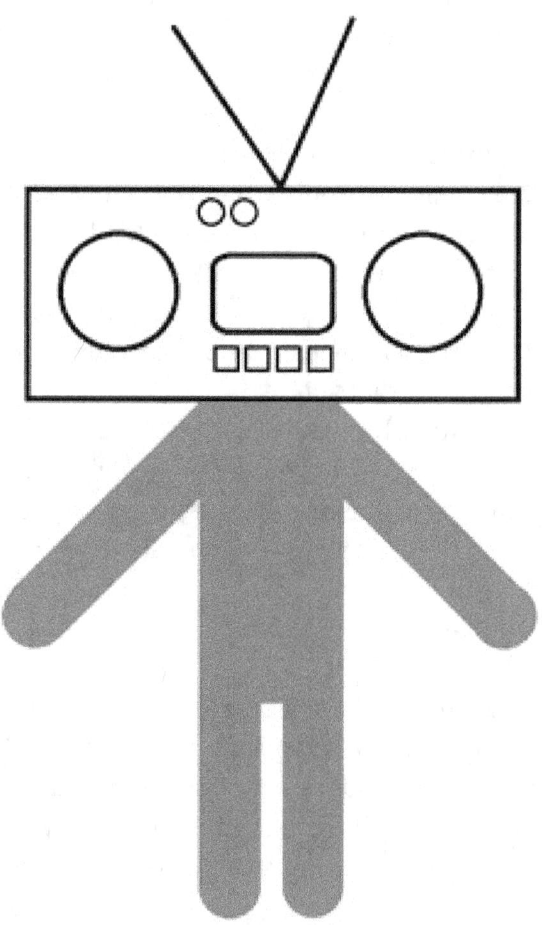

Visualization Mad Libs

Find a/an ________________ position, either sitting or lying
      (relaxing adjective)

down, and close your eyes. Take a few deep breaths and relax

the muscles in your ________________. Imagine you are
      (body part that feels tense)

standing in a/an ________________ ________________. You
      (adjective)   *(place)*

feel very ________________ and safe. As you look around, you
     (positive emotion)

notice there are many ________________. The weather is
     (something you like)

________________, and your whole body feels ________________.
(type of weather)   *(relaxing adjective)*

You notice a ________________ ________________ has
     (color)   *(animal)*

approached you. It looks friendly and ________________, and
      (positive adjective)

it tells you that you are ________________ and ________________.
     (positive adjective) *(positive adjective)*

It says that it loves your ________________, and it wants to
     (personal quality)

always keep you safe and happy. It tells you that, any time

you feel _________________, you can come back to this place
      (negative emotion)

and listen to it tell you all the great things about yourself.

Take some more deep breaths and think about how many

people care about you and think you are _______________.
                                    (positive adjective)

As you open your eyes, notice how _______________ you feel.
                     (positive emotion)

Remember that you can come back to this _______________
                                    (positive adjective)

place any time you feel _______________.
              (negative emotion)

Happy Thoughts

Feelings and thoughts are tied together. When we feel happy, we tend to think happy thoughts. When we feel sad, we think sad thoughts. And when we feel mad, our brains fill up with angry thoughts. This is why a lot of kids will ruminate when they are in a bad mood.

The good news is, our thoughts do not just follow our feelings—our feelings follow our thoughts, too! So when a child is having a negative feeling, deliberately thinking positive thoughts can bring their mood up. The activities in this section help them to focus on positive thoughts to bring up their mood.

Do Not Think About Pink Elephants

You have thoughts all the time, even when you're not paying attention to them. Some of these thoughts are about people, some are about things you will do or have done, some are about yourself, and some are just random. Sometimes thoughts pop into your head, and you don't have control over the things you think. This is all normal!

Let's try an experiment. Whatever you do, no matter what, for the next 10 seconds, ***DO NOT THINK ABOUT PINK ELEPHANTS.*** You can think about anything else that you want, but ***DO NOT THINK ABOUT PINK ELEPHANTS.***

...What were you thinking about? I bet it was pink elephants. That's because you can't just tell yourself *not* to think about something—you have to replace a thought with another one.

On the next page, write or draw something that makes you feel calm, happy, or relaxed. It can be a place, song, person, or anything else you can imagine. Include as much detail as you can—colors, shapes, feelings, sounds, anything else you can think of. Then, when you have a bad thought, simply tell yourself, "I am choosing to think about my happy thought instead." Focus on your happy thing to make the bad thought go away!

Do Not Think About Pink Elephants

My Bad Mood Journal

You can use this journal any time you are in a very bad mood and need some support. This will help you remember to use your skills to notice your feelings, communicate them to others, and, when you're ready, bring yourself into a more positive mood.

Right now, I feel: _______________________________________

Did something happen that caused my mood to change?

____

____

____

Where in my body am I holding my feelings?

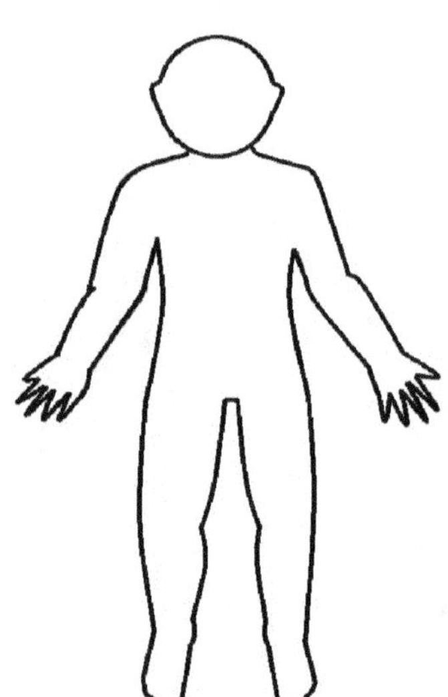

What does this feeling feel like in my body?

This feeling makes me want to:

____

____

____

____

It's okay to feel this way! What are sine choices I can make
that will help me with this feeling but won't get me into
trouble? Draw or write them in the hearts.

When I am ready to have happier thoughts, here is what I
will think about:

When my mood is better, here is how I will show people how
I am feeling now:

____

____

____

____

93

I Am Grateful For

You Can Wish Happy Wishes!

You can wish happy wishes out into th eworld any time you want to! They can be about one specific person or thing, a group of people, an event happening, or just for the whole world. Just think about the wishes, like shooting stars, and imagine sending them to whoever you want!

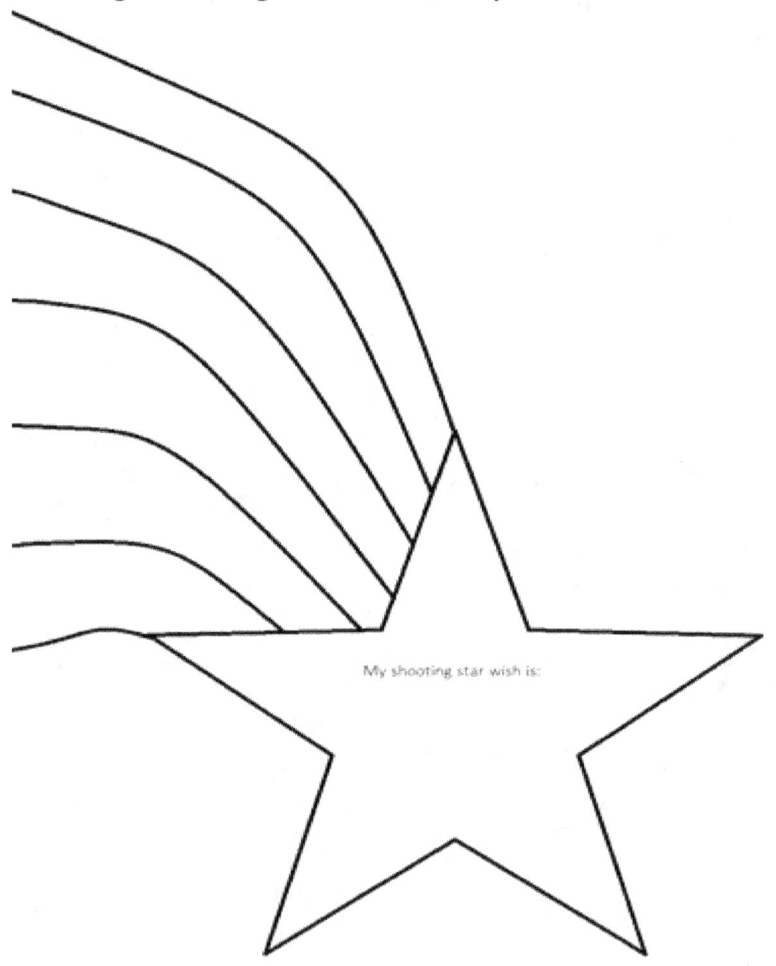

My Coping Skills Toolbox

Now that you have learned many different ways to share and cope with your feelings, you can think about the ways that worked best for you. This will help you make a plan for how to deal with different feelings before they occur. That way, you can make better choices in the moment! You can use these pages to list skills that help you most with different feelings, or put together a folder or kit that you can use any time you need some help.

Remember, everyone has hard feelings sometimes, and we all need to ask for help. It's okay to have a hard day, and everyone makes mistakes sometimes. Your toolbox is meant to help you deal with feelings so you can make better choices no matter how you are feeling!

What helps me when I feel sad?	What helps me when I feel angry?

| What helps me when I feel scared? | What helps me when I feel hyper? |

| What helps me when I feel _____________? | What helps me when I feel _____________? |

THANK YOU FOR BRINGING ME ON YOUR JOURNEY!

If you enjoyed this book, I'd be very grateful if you'd post a short review on Amazon.

For more resources, check out my website: www.dramymarschall.com.

You can also follow me on Facebook (www.facebook.com/dramymarschall) and Twitter (@DrAmyMarschall).

Thanks again for your support!